Trivia of the Silver Screen

by
Lester Gordon

SANTA MONICA PRESS
P.O. Box 1076
Santa Monica, CA 90406-1076
Printed in the United States
All Rights Reserved

Contents

Trivia about Actors

Rudolph Valentino's real name was Rodolfo Alfonzo Pierre Philibert Guglielmi d'Antonguolla.

Kevin Costner almost got his big break in Lawrence Kasdan's yuppie hit *The Big Chill*. The movie was about a group of old college buddies getting together to mourn the death of their friend, Alex. Alex was played by Costner, and he originally had a fairly large role. But at the last minute Kasdan decided to edit him completely out of the movie! To make it up to him, several years later Kasdan hired Costner to play a gunfighter in his hit western *Silverado*.

It took many years for Humphrey Bogart to break into Hollywood. While he was still a struggling actor, he made a living by playing professional chess.

Before moving to New York to try his luck on Broadway, Paul Newman lived in Cleveland. He helped out the rest of his family in running a small sporting goods store.

To date, Paul Newman has donated over 65 million dollars to charities for terminally ill children. He raises the funds for this worthwhile cause through the sale of his "Newman's Own" brand of foods in grocery stores across the country.

Gregory Peck was not able to enlist in the United States armed forces in World War II due to a spinal injury. As a result, his career soared during the war years, because other stars, like Clark Gable and Jimmy Stewart, were in Europe fighting against the Germans.

Contrary to popular belief, movie hunk Mel Gibson is not actually Australian. He was born in New York City, but he moved to the Land Down Under when he was very young. Some of his earliest roles were in Australian movies such as *Galipoli* and *Mad Max*.

Marlon Brando is quite a recluse. He lives on a private island in the South Pacific with his family and housekeepers.

John Wayne was nicknamed Duke by his friends because that was the name of Wayne's boyhood dog. Wayne's real name was Marion Michael Morrison.

Humphrey Bogart was so short that he had to wear platform shoes during the filming of *Casablanca* in order to appear as tall as Ingrid Bergman.

Spencer Tracy is the only actor to ever receive an Academy Award with the wrong name engraved on it. Instead of reading "Spencer Tracy," the award read "Dick Tracy!"

Nicholas Cage (*Honeymoon in Vegas, Peggy Sue Got Married*) is director Francis Ford Coppola's nephew.

Can you believe that anyone would turn down a marriage proposal from a handsome and charming star like Cary Grant? Sophia Loren did just that in 1957, when Grant proposed to her during the filming of *The Pride and the Passion*.

Before becoming a successful actor, Harrison Ford worked as a carpenter. His last carpentry job ended just a few days before filming on *Star Wars* began.

Gene Hackman and Dustin Hoffman were both students at a legendary acting school called the Actor's Playhouse. The two were voted the least likely to succeed in their acting careers!

John Barrymore was the first actor to play Dr. Jekyll and Mr. Hyde in the movies. He had such accurate control of his facial muscles that he was able to perform the famous transformation scenes without any makeup!

Humphrey Bogart was originally going to become a surgeon, following in the footsteps of his father, but he was expelled from a medical school for disciplinary reasons.

Bogart spoke with his trademark lisp due to an accident he suffered in the navy. He caught a tiny piece of shrapnel in his upper lip, leaving some scarring and a slight speech impediment.

Apart from being a fine actor, James Stewart is an accomplished accordian player and poet.

Marlon Brando has a reputation for being a very difficult actor to work with. For example, when he appeared in *The Freshmen*, a comedy starring Matthew Broderick, he refused to memorize his lines! The producers overcame this problem by giving his character a hearing aid. Someone off-camera read his lines into a microphone, which he could hear through the hearing aid, and Brando then repeated the lines for the camera.

Sean Connery's real name is Thomas Connery.

Sean Connery ran away from home and joined the navy at the age of 15. Upon leaving the armed forces, he was able to gain employment as a swimsuit model, due to his muscular physique.

Gary Cooper held several jobs before becoming an actor. His father, a supreme court justice for the state of Montana, insisted that he study the law. As a result, Cooper worked as an attorney for a brief period. He then discovered his uncanny ability to draw caricatures, resulting in his moving to Los Angeles to become a political cartoonist. Finding the cartooning world hard to break into, however, he earned a living by acting as an extra in Hollywood movies. A big-time Hollywood producer subsequently decided to give him a starring role in *The Winning of Barbara Worth*. The rest is history.

Pee Wee Herman's real name is Paul Reubens.

One of Tom Cruise's first starring roles was in Francis Coppola's film adaptation of the S.E. Hinton novel *The Outsiders*. This movie also featured such future stars as Matt Dillon, Ralph Macchio, Emilio Estevez, Patrick Swayze, and C. Thomas Howell.

Robert De Niro's parents pushed him into becoming an actor in order to keep him off the streets at night. De Niro was a wild youth, belonging to a gang and committing several petty crimes. Most acting lessons take place at night, so De Niro's parents felt that he could spend his evenings more constructively by learning a trade.

James Dean's mother died while he was still quite young. His father, a hard-working dentist, did not have enough time to take care of the boy. As a result, Dean grew up under the guardianship of his aunt and uncle in Iowa.

As well as acting, Clint Eastwood has followed a career in politics. He served two terms as the mayor of Carmel, a small town in northern California.

Henry Fonda is the direct descendent of some of the first Dutch settlers of New York. In fact, there is a town in New York named Fonda.

Henry Fonda studied acting under Marlon Brando's mother.

Harrison Ford's wife, Melissa Matheson, wrote *E.T.: The Extra-Terrestrial*.

Clark Gable decided to join the Army Air Corps during World War II due to the extreme grief that he was feeling over the premature death of his wife, Carole Lombard. He flew in almost fifty bombing missions over Germany.

Everyone knows that Tarzan was quite an athlete, but few people realize that Johnny Weissmueller, the actor who played him in the 1930s, was an athlete too. Weissmueller won several gold medals swimming in the Olympics.

Mel Gibson is a very quiet and religious man. He is a devoted father of six, and he spends most of his free time at home with his family on their ranch in southern Australia.

Cary Grant led a very hectic private life. He was ridiculed for his belief in the supernatural, and one of his many divorces involved public accusations of his being addicted to LSD.

Gene Hackman ran away from home and joined the Marines when he was sixteen years old.

Dustin Hoffman, Gene Hackman, and Robert Duvall were all roommates at one time.

Eddie Murphy became a household name when he was just nineteen years old. He was the hottest new star of *Saturday Night Live*, and it would take only two more years for him to star in his first feature film, *48 Hours*.

In 1989, Art Buchwald sued Eddie Murphy for allegedly stealing the plot to the film *Coming to America*.

Paul Newman attended graduate school at Yale University.

Jack Nicholson earned some $60 million dollars for his portrayal of the Joker in

Batman. Most of this was not due to his salary, but to the profits he received from the sales of all *Batman* merchandise.

Robert Redford's love for baseball goes back much further than his starring role in Barry Levinson's *The Natural*. Redford has played baseball all his life, and his skill at the sport enabled him to win an athletic scholarship to attend the University of Colorado.

Burt Reynolds is one-fourth Native American, his paternal grandmother being a full-blooded Cherokee.

Burt Reynold's father was the chief of police of the small town in which they lived.

John Wayne smoked five packs of cigarettes a day for almost 25 years. He died of lung cancer in 1979.

Arnold Schwarzenegger won the Mr. Universe competition three times and the Mr. Olympia competition seven times.

Before he became a star, Arnold Schwarzenegger went by the stage name "Arnold Strong."

While he was still a young man, Bob Hope aspired to be a boxer.

Sylvester Stallone attended the American College in Switzerland on an athletic scholarship. While there, he worked as the coach of the girl's soccer team.

One of Sylvester Stallone's first movie roles was as a thug on a New York subway train in Woody Allen's hysterical *Bananas*. The last shot we see of Stallone in that movie is him beating Woody Allen over the head with an old woman's crutch!

James Stewart attended Princeton University and studied architecture.

While still fresh out of college, James Stewart joined a theater company whose cast included Henry Fonda.

Trivia about Actresses

Almost 1,500 different actresses sent in their resumes to play the part of Scarlett O'Hara in David O. Selznick's legendary production of *Gone with the Wind*. Of this 1,500, almost 500 had actual auditions. But in the end, the role went to Vivien Leigh, who was the producer's top choice right from the beginning!

Lauren Bacall's real name is Bette Joan Perske.

Talia Shire is director Francis Ford Coppola's sister. She has appeared in such hits as *Rocky* and *The Godfather*. Her son is Nicholas Cage.

Judy Garland's real name was Frances Gumm. She made her show business debut with her two siblings in a singing group known as the Gumm Sisters. Her father hoped that all three of his daughters would be discovered by Hollywood, but only Frances went on to great fame.

To get an idea of who the public would like to see playing Scarlett O'Hara in the movie version of *Gone with the Wind*, producers ran ads in newspapers across the country inviting anyone to write in with suggestions. Only one person suggested Vivien Leigh!

Lauren Bacall shied away from the limelight and put her acting career on hold from 1951 to 1957, as she nursed her husband, Humphrey Bogart, through his fatal battle with cancer.

While still just a teenager, Lauren Bacall was a covergirl model for *Harper's Bazaar*.

Cher's real name is Cherilyn Sarkisian.

Although Cher was best known as a singer before her acting career took off in the 1980s, she had appeared in almost twenty films throughout the '60s and '70s.

Joan Crawford's real name was Lucille Fay Le Sueur.

One year after Joan Crawford's death in 1977, her daughter published a biography which accused Crawford of being an abusive mother. This book, entitled *Mommie Dearest*, was made into a film starring Faye Dunaway.

Everyone loves Marilyn Monroe's famous scene in *The Seven Year Itch* (in which she stands over a subway grating, and the hot air lifts up her skirt). Everyone, that is, except Joe Dimaggio, her husband at the time. He was so embarrassed by the scene that he filed for a divorce just a few weeks after the film opened. (Good thing he never married Sharon Stone!)

Bette Davis was working as an actress in off-Broadway plays while still a teenager. During one of her shows, acclaimed director George Cukor commented that she would never make it in Hollywood due to her looks. Undaunted, she set out to prove Cukor wrong, and she found herself hired by Universal Studios at the tender age of twenty-three.

Geena Davis began her career in show business as a fashion model. Her first screen role was as a soap opera actress in *Tootsie*.

Jane Fonda studied art while attending college in France.

Jane Fonda's first show business job was as a fashion model.

Jodie Foster's career in show business started when she was just two years old. She modeled as the "Coppertone baby" in various advertisements. She has been acting non-stop since then, appearing in such acclaimed movies as *Taxi Driver* and *Silence of the Lambs*. Foster has already won two Academy Awards.

Howard Hughes, aviator and movie mogul, was once romantically involved with actress Jane Russell. Ms. Russell had a healthy bust line, which Hughes realized was a selling point in her movies. As a result, he put his engineering skills to the test and designed a bra specifically to make her look *even* better endowed! The bra was an unqualified success. The Hayes Commission, however, was not so happy about it. This commission served as Hollywood's rating system and censorship board until the 1950s, and they felt that Ms. Russell's bust should be toned down, not augmented.

John Hinckley attempted to assassinate President Ronald Reagan in order to impress Jodie Foster. Hinckley had been in love with the actress since she was a child.

Katharine Hepburn's mother was an outspoken advocate of birth control.

Katharine Hepburn had a romantic relationship with Spencer Tracy that lasted almost thrity years. Although the two were never married, when Tracy became very ill in the mid-1960s, Hepburn put her career on hold in order to nurse him back to health.

Katharine Hepburn's only marriage was to a man named Ludlow Ogden Smith. The marriage was an unqualified failure, as it lasted less than a month.

Katharine Hepburn has won four Academy Awards, more than any other actress to this day. The films for which she won awards are *Guess Who's Coming to Dinner, The Lion in Winter, Morning Glory*, and *On Golden Pond*.

Jessica Lange studied acting and pantomime in France. While there, she worked as a chorus dancer in the *Opera Comique*.

Marilyn Monroe's real name was Norma Jean Mortenson.

Marilyn Monroe was sexually abused by several of her mother's boyfriends while she was still just a child.

Marilyn Monroe worked at an aircraft plant before breaking into the field of modeling.

Upon first moving to Los Angeles from her home town of Santa Ana, Michelle Pfeiffer quickly fell in with the wrong crowd. She was conned into joining a cult, and she was not able to free herself for several years.

Susan Sarandon's real name is Susan Tomaling.

Meryl Streep appeared in over forty plays while still a graduate student at Yale University.

One of Barbra Streisand's earliest jobs was as a switchboard operator.

Sigourney Weaver grew up in a show business family. Her mother was a working actress, and her father was the president of the NBC television network.

Debra Winger, one of the most acclaimed actresses working today, got her first screen role as Lynda Carter's little sister on TV's *Wonder Woman!*

Trivia about Directors

Quentin Tarantino, who is now riding the wave of his success from the cult hits *Reservoir Dogs* and *Pulp Fiction*, did not study directing in film school. Rather, he learned his craft simply by watching as many movies as possible. Prior to becoming a Hollywood big-shot, Tarantino worked the night shift in a 24-hour video store. One of the perks of his job was free movie rentals!

Quentin Tarantino once amassed over $5,000 worth of parking tickets. Needless to say, on a video store clerk's salary, he could not pay the fine. A few days before he was scheduled to go to court, however, he received word that he would be able to direct his debut feature, *Reservoir Dogs*. Within a few days, he had signed the deal that would make him a millionaire!

Woody Allen's real name is Allen Stewart Konigsberg.

Prior to becoming a film director, Woody Allen was a highly successful stand-up comedian and joke writer for *The Tonight Show*.

John Ford was an extra in D.W. Griffith's acclaimed silent epic *The Birth of a Nation*.

John Ford won four Academy Awards for directing, a record that still stands to this day. The films for which he won the awards are *The Grapes of Wrath*, *How Green Was My Valley*, *The Informer*, and *The Quiet Man*.

When Alfred Hitchcock was a child, his father punished him by having the police throw him in jail overnight.

George Lucas has only directed three movies: *THX 1138*, *American Grafitti*, and *Star Wars*. He acted as a producer on all other films bearing his name.

Frank Capra studied chemical engineering at the California Institute of Technology at Pasadena.

During World War II, Capra decided to support the United States' war effort by making a series of documentaries about the need to fight against the Germans. The series was called simply *Why We Fight*.

Francis Ford Coppola is an avid wine lover, and he even owns a vineyard in California's lush Napa valley. When he is not directing, Coppola likes to spend time overseeing the workings of the vineyard.

Francis Ford Coppola's grandfather was one of the inventors of the Vitaphone, an early type of record player.

D.W. Griffith invented the false eyelash for his film *Intolerance*.

D.W. Griffith was the first director ever to take a percentage of net revenues from a picture instead of a salary. He did so for his epic *The Birth of a Nation*, making him one of America's earliest multi-millionaires.

Roger Corman studied mechanical engineering at Stanford University.

Roger Corman started his career in Hollywood as a lowly messenger boy.

Fewer than 100 of Hollywood's major films have been directed by women.

John Singleton was the first African American ever to be nominated for an Academy Award for Best Director.

John Ford's real name is Sean Aloysius O'Feeney.

John Ford directed over fifty films during his long career.

John Ford was so fierce about his independence as an artist that he would go so far as to burn any footage that he did not want to put into the movie. That way, the studio could not re-edit his films.

Alfred Hitchcock attended the School of Engineering and Navigation in London.

While there, he studied mechanics and navigation.

Alfred Hitchcock's first job in the film industry was as a title card painter (title cards were the written dialogue that the audience could read between scenes in silent movies).

Stanley Kubrick is a major recluse, much in the same fashion as acclaimed author J.D. Salinger. Kubrick lives in a small castle somewhere in England. The castle is surrounded by a mote. He grants very few interviews, and there are almost no known pictures of him in circulation today. He never leaves England, filming all of his movies there (for *Full Metal Jacket*, a film about the War in Vietnam, he even imported palm trees into Great Britain in order to accurately re-create the terrain of Southeast Asia!).

When people hear the name Akira Kurosawa, they generally think of Samurai films. But few people realize that Kurosawa has a great love for Western art, especially Shakespeare. In fact, *Ran* and *Throne of Blood*, two of his most famous works, are based on Shakespeare plays.

When he was growing up in the small town of Modesto, California, George Lucas was passionately in love with cars. He wanted to become a race car driver after graduating from high school. But just a few days before his graduation, he got into a terrible car crash in his little Fiat, forever ending his love affair with the automobile. The crash was so severe that Lucas was actually thrown from his vehicle, which came to a halt after it hit a tree.

Directors will go to great lengths to ensure that their actors give realistic and spontaneous performances. When directing *Casablanca*, for example, Michael Curtiz pretended that he did not know how the movie would end. He claimed that the ending was still being rewritten. So, when the fateful day came to film the parting scene between Rick and Ilsa, no one but Curtiz knew whether Ingrid Bergman was going to get on the plane or stay with Bogey!

Martin Scorsese originally studied to be a Catholic priest.

Ridley Scott started his career in the film industry as a set designer.

Steven Spielberg's father was a pioneer in the computer industry. He invented some of the first transistor chips for computers.

Steven Spielberg started making movies when he was just six years old. He took his family's 8mm camera with him wherever he went, and he liked to direct tiny little war epics that starred his friends. Spielberg directed his first feature-length movie when he was sixteen. He funded the work by mowing people's lawns. He even managed to convince a local movie theater owner to let him show the movie, called *Firelight*, on two consecutive nights.

Despite all of Steven Spielberg's amazing talent and experience at film-making during his youth, no major film school would accept him. His high school grades were too poor!

Today Oliver Stone is known as one of the most out-spoken critics of the War in Vietnam. But few people realize that he actually *volunteered* to serve in that war; he was not drafted.

Orson Welles was the son of a wealthy couple in Kenosha, Wisconsin. By the time he was fifteen, both of his parents had died, so he traveled to England to study the theater. His talent was so great that, by the following year, he was already directing Shakespeare plays for the Royal Shakespeare Company (one of the most prestigious theater groups in the world!). Two short years later, he was performing on Broadway.

Orson Welles once sent the entire country into a panic state when he broadcast *The War of the Worlds* over the radio. He gave the classic H.G. Welles story a new slant by retelling it in a documentary style, as if the alien invasion were actually occurring. Unfortunately, most of the listeners did not realize that this was simply a piece of fiction, and they thought the world really was about to come to an end!

Stanley Kubrick was such a perfectionist that he insisted on shooting *Barry Lyndon*, a period piece starring Ryan O'Neil, by candle light. He claimed that candles were the only indoor light source during the period when the movie took place, so candles should be the only indoor light source during the making of the movie! The only problem was that no lens existed that was sensitive enough to shoot by candle light. With the help of NASA, the director of photography had to invent one.

Who has directed more films than anyone else? The late William Beaudine can lay claim to that honor, having directed 128 shorts, 144 talking features, and 32 silent features.

It took four directors to make *Twilight Zone, the Movie*: Joe Dante, John Landis, George Miller and Steven Spielberg.

Famed silent comedy director Fatty Arbuckle was once accused of killing an actress. Although the charges proved to be groundless, he was still ostracized by the film-going public. In order to continue making movies, he had to adopt a number of different pseudonyms.

Fatty Arbuckle helped Charlie Chaplin design the latter's famed hobo costume. Arbuckle's contribution: the baggy pants were his (they didn't call him Fatty for nothing!).

Steven Spielberg holds the distinction of starting a new merit badge for the Boy Scouts of America—film-making.

Milos Forman, the celebrated director of such films as *One Flew Over the Cuckoo's Nest* and *Valmont*, defected from Communist Czechoslovakia during the late 1960s. When he directed *Amadeus*, about the life of Mozart, he discovered that some crucial locations were now in Communist territory. After pulling many strings, Forman was allowed to return to his homeland to shoot the movie. He was the only defector from a Communist country ever to be allowed to return to that country without going to jail!

Who is the worst director of all time? That distinction would have to go to Allen Smithee. The only problem is, Mr. Smithee is not just one man. You see, the Director's Guild of America has very strict rules about the use of pseudonyms. Any time that a director is embarrassed about his or her own work, and they want to use a pseudonym to hide their involvement on a project, they have to be careful not to accidentally besmirch the name of another member of the Guild. As a result, the Guild invented the name "Allen Smithee." No one in the Guild has this name, so any director may claim it at any time!

Noteable Quotes

"It's hard work making movies. It's like being a doctor—you work long hours, very hard hours, and it's emotional, tense work. If you don't really love it, then it ain't worth it."
—George Lucas

"I have decided that while I am a star I will be every inch and every moment a star. Everyone from the studio gateman to the highest executive will know it."
—Gloria Swanson

"Hollywood is a sewer—with service from the Ritz Carlton."
—Wilson Mizner

"She just plain wore out."
—Roy Bolger on the death of Judy Garland

"The next time I send a damn fool for something, I go myself."
—Michael Curtiz

"They've got great respect for the dead in Hollywood, but none for the living!"
—Erroll Flynn

"He's the kind of guy that, when he dies, he's going up to Heaven and giving God a bad time for making him bald."
—Marlon Brando on Frank Sinatra

"He's just another California blonde."
—Screenwriter William Goldman on Robert Redford

"You really like me!"
—Sally Field accepting her second Oscar in 1984

"From what I hear about Communism, I don't like it, because it isn't on the level."
—Gary Cooper

"Hollywood stinks."
—Frank Sinatra

"It took longer to make one of Mary's [Pickford's] contracts than it did to make one of Mary's movies."
—Sam Goldwyn on the business side of Hollywood

"A good director doesn't get in the way of a script. That's all a good director does."
—William Goldman

"A director's job is to make the actors comfortable enough to perform to their best abilities."
—Clint Eastwood

"Hollywood is a place where they'll pay you $50,000 for a kiss and 50 cents for your soul."
—Marilyn Monroe

"There is a disagreement between the way things are and the way I think things should be."
—Francis Ford Coppola

"When I was a child, I remember the church had on display lists of films, in categories "A," "B," and "C." "C" meant it was condemned by the Legion of Decency. If you walked into a theater showing that film and you had a heart attack, you're in Hell. If you went to see a Max Ophuls film, you were finished."
—Martin Scorsese

"Behind every successful man there stands an astonished woman."
—Frank Capra

"Hollywood's a place where they shoot too many pictures and not enough actors."
—Walter Winchell

"I love movies. It's my whole life and that's it."
—Martin Scorsese

"[Orson Welles] is at heart a magician whose particular talent lies not so much in his creative imagination—which is considerable—but in his proven ability to stretch the familiar elements of theatrical effect far beyond their normal point of tension."
—John Houseman

"This year, I'm a star, but what will I be next year? A black hole?"
—Woody Allen

"He's one of the best. He's outwitted the empire on numerous occasions, and he's

41

made some very fast deals. One of his problems is that he gambles quite heavily and that's where he loses most of his money. He's tough and sharp, only somehow he never manages to scrape together enough to get any power."
—George Lucas on the similarities between Han Solo and Francis Ford Coppola

"Pictures are the only business where you can sit out front and applaud yourself."
—Will Rogers

"Making a film is a cross between a circus, a military campaign, a nightmare, and an orgy."
—Norman Mailer

"Movie making is like sex. You start doing it, and then you get interested in getting better at it."
—Norman Mailer

"This is one of the most fortuitous tricks in the history of civilization: that the greatest living villain in the world and the

greatest comedian should look alike."
—Douglas Fairbanks on the similarities between Adoplh Hitler and Charlie Chaplin

"The script is what you've dreamed up—this is what [the film] should be. The film is what you end up with."
—George Lucas

"Give the people what they want, they'll all show up."
—Red Skelton

"I have a sneaking suspicion that if there were a way to make movies without actors, [directors] would do it."
—Mark Hammill

"Hollywood is where, if you don't have happiness, you send out for it."
—Rex Reed

"Movies are more than they are just by virtue of being on film. I think a film can be easily more than the people who made it."
—Mike Nichols

"Didn't you see those big ears when you talked to him, and those big feet and hands, not to mention that ugly face of his?"
—Jack Warner lamenting over Clark Gable's screen test

"I don't make pictures just to make money. I make money to make more pictures."
—Walt Disney

"Failure has a thousand explanations. Success doesn't need one."
—Alec Guiness

"Making movies is an apprenticeship for life."
—Robert Watts

"You can take all the sincerity in Hollywood, place it in the navel of a fruit fly, and still have enough room for three caraway seeds and a producer's heart."
—Fred Allen

The Most Popular Actors, Actresses, and Movies

Each year, a poll is taken with the owners of movie theaters to determine which actor and which actress was most popular with their audiences. In order to be as objective as possible, the theater owners make their determinations based upon ticket sales. This poll is called the Quigley poll. It has existed since 1915, and the results are listed below by year.

1915—William S. Hart, Mary Pickford
1916—William S. Hart, Mary Pickford
1917—Douglas Fairbanks, Anita Stewart
1918—Douglas Fairbanks, Mary Pickford
1919—Wallace Reid, Mary Pickford
1920—Wallace Reid, Marguerite Clark
1921—Douglas Fairbanks, Mary Pickford
1922—Douglas Fairbanks, Mary Pickford
1923—Thomas Meighan, Norma
      Talmadge
1924—Rudolph Valentino, Norma
      Talmadge
1925—Rudolph Valentino, Norma
      Talmadge
1926—Tom Mix, Colleen Moore
1927—Tom Mix, Colleen Moore
1928—Lon Chaney, Clara Bow

1929—Lon Chaney, Clara Bow
1930—William Haines, Joan Crawford
1931—Charles Farrell, Janet Gaynor
1932—Charles Farrell, Marie Dressler
1933—Will Rogers, Marie Dressler
1934—Will Rogers, Janet Gaynor
1935—Will Rogers, Shirley Temple
1936—Clark Gable, Shirley Temple
1937—Clark Gable, Shirley Temple
1938—Mickey Rooney, Shirley Temple
1939—Mickey Rooney, Shirley Temple
1940—Mickey Rooney, Bette Davis
1941—Mickey Rooney, Bette Davis
1942—Bud Abbott/Lou Costello, Betty
      Grable
1943—Bob Hope, Betty Grable
1944—Bing Crosby, Betty Grable
1945—Bing Crosby, Greer Garson
1946—Bing Crosby, Ingrid Bergman
1947—Bing Crosby, Betty Grable
1948—Bing Crosby, Betty Grable
1949—Bob Hope, Betty Grable
1950—John Wayne, Betty Grable
1951—John Wayne, Betty Grable
1952—Dean Martin/Jerry Lewis, Betty
      Grable
1953—Gary Cooper, Marilyn Monroe

1954—John Wayne, Marilyn Monroe
1955—James Stewart, Grace Kelly
1956—William Holden, Marilyn Monroe
1957—Rock Hudson, Kim Novak
1958—Glenn Ford, Elizabeth Taylor
1959—Rock Hudson, Doris Day
1960—Rock Hudson, Doris Day
1961—Rock Hudson, Elizabeth Taylor
1962—Rock Hudson, Doris Day
1963—John Wayne, Doris Day
1964—Jack Lemmon, Doris Day
1965—Sean Connery, Doris Day
1966—Sean Connery, Julie Andrews
1967—Lee Marvin, Julie Andrews
1968—Sidney Poitier, Julie Andrews
1969—Paul Newman, Katharine
      Hepburn
1970—Paul Newman, Barbra Streisand
1971—John Wayne, Ali MacGraw
1972—Clint Eastwood, Barbra Streisand
1973—Clint Eastwood, Barbra Streisand
1974—Robert Redford, Barbra Streisand
1975—Robert Redford, Barbra Streisand
1976—Robert Redford, Tatum O'Neal
1977—Sylvester Stallone, Barbra
      Streisand
1978—Burt Reynolds, Diane Keaton

1979—Burt Reynolds, Jane Fonda
1980—Burt Reynolds, Jane Fonda
1981—Burt Reynolds, Dolly Parton
1982—Burt Reynolds, Dolly Parton
1983—Clint Eastwood, Meryl Streep
1984—Clint Eastwood, Sally Field
1985—Sylvester Stallone, Meryl Streep
1986—Tom Cruise, Bette Midler
1987—Eddie Murphy, Glenn Close
1988—Tom Cruise, Bette Midler
1989—Jack Nicholson, Kathleen Turner
1990—Arnold Schwarzenegger, Julia
          Roberts
1991—Arnold Schwarzenegger, Jodie
          Foster
1992—Jack Nicholson, Demi Moore
1993—Tom Hanks, Angela Bassett
1994—Tom Hanks, Jodie Foster

Since 1947, *Variety* magazine has kept accurate records regarding how much money has been earned by movies within the United States. Each year, they present an award to the film which earned the most money. The winners of that award are as follows:

1947—*The Best Years of Our Lives*
1948—*The Road to Rio*
1949—*Jolson Sings Again*
1950—*Samson and Delilah*
1951—*David and Bathsheba*
1952—*The Greatest Show on Earth*
1953—*The Robe*
1954—*White Christmas*
1955—*Cinerama Holiday*
1956—*Guys and Dolls*
1957—*The Ten Commandments*
1958—*The Bridge on the River Kwai*
1959—*Auntie Mame*
1960—*Ben Hur*
1961—*The Guns of Navarone*
1962—*Spartacus*
1963—*Cleopatra*
1964—*The Carpetbaggers*
1965—*Mary Poppins*
1966—*Thunderball*
1967—*The Dirty Dozen*
1968—*The Graduate*
1969—*The Love Bug*
1970—*Airport*
1971—*Love Story*
1972—*The Godfather*
1973—*The Poseidon Adventure*
1974—*The Sting*

1975—*Jaws*
1976—*One Flew Over the Cuckoo's Nest*
1977—*Star Wars*
1978—*Grease*
1979—*Superman*
1980—*The Empire Strikes Back*
1981—*Raiders of the Lost Ark*
1982—*E.T.: The Extra-Terrestrial*
1983—*Return of the Jedi*
1984—*Ghostbusters*
1985—*Back to the Future*
1986—*Top Gun*
1987—*Beverly Hills Cop II*
1988—*Who Framed Roger Rabbit*
1989—*Batman*
1990—*Ghost*
1991—*Terminator 2: Judgment Day*
1992—*A Few Good Men*
1993—*Jurassic Park*
1994—*Forrest Gump*

While we are on the subject of money and movies, let's take a look at the most expensive movies of all time:

1) *Waterworld*—$175,000,000
2) *True Lies*—$120,000,000

3) *Terminator 2: Judgment Day*—
    $104,000,000
4) *Die Hard With a Vengeance*—
    $80,000,000
5) *Who Framed Roger Rabbit*—
    $70,000,000
6) *The Last Action Hero*—$67,000,000
7) *Jurassic Park*—$65,000,000
8) *Total Recall*—$64,000,000
9) *Rambo III*—$63,000,000
10) *Die Harder*—$62,000,000
11) *Judge Dredd*—$60,000,000
12) *Godfather III*—$60,000,000
13) *Batman Forever*—$60,000,000
14) *Superman*—$55,000,000
15) *The Fugitive*—$50,000,000
16) *Batman Returns*—$45,000,000
17) *Cleopatra*—$44,000,000
18) *Batman*—$40,000,000
19) *Indiana Jones and the Last Crusade*—
    $36,000,000
20) *Return of the Jedi*—$35,000,000
21) *The Empire Strikes Back*—
    $30,000,000
22) *Indiana Jones and the Temple of
    Doom*—$25,000,000
23) *Raiders of the Lost Ark*—$20,000,000

A British periodical named *Time Out* once invited some of the most respected directors in the world to choose their fifty favorite movies. The following is the list that they compiled:

Citizen Kane
The Third Man
The Night of the Hunter
Some Like it Hot
The Godfather
Vertigo
L'Atalante
Raging Bull
Children of Paradise
North by Northwest
Once Upon a Time in the West
Touch of Evil
Rules of the Game
Psycho
The Wizard of Oz
Blue Velvet
Apocalypse Now
Chinatown
A Matter of Life and Death
The Searchers
Tokyo Story
Brazil

Kiss Me Deadly
Sweet Smell of Success
Beauty and the Beast
Once Upon a Time in America
Don't Look Now
Rear Window
The Life and Death of Colonel Blimp
The Big Sleep
Notorious
A Streetcar Named Desire
The American Friend
The Magnificent Ambersons
The Tree of Wooden Clogs
Singin' in the Rain
The King of Comedy
Bonnie and Clyde
Jean de Florette
Kind Hearts and Coronettes
Mean Streets
Seven Samurai
Written on the Wind
Gospel According to Saint Matthew
Double Indemnity
Ivan the Terrible
Red Balloon
The Passion of Joan of Arc
Out of the Past
Earth

Hooray for Hollywood!

The "Hollywood" sign that stands atop Los Angeles was first built in 1923. Few people realize this, but the sign originally said "Hollywoodland." The letters were made out of metal and stood some fifty feet tall, and light bulbs were placed around the perimeter of each. This sign caused an excessive amount of glare on nearby freeways, however, so it was quickly replaced with the sign with which we are all now familiar. Each letter cost almost $30,000 to erect, and the sign became a national landmark in 1973. For many years a caretaker of the sign resided in the second L!

There is a famous movie theater in Hollywood called Grauman's Chinese Theater. This is where the stars go to have their handprints and footprints permanently recorded in cement. The first star to do so was named Norma Talmadge. Some people assert that she simply walked into some wet cement by mistake, thereby starting a trend that continues to this day.

The stars that line Hollywood Boulevard in Hollywood are collectively called the walk of fame. There are just over 2,500 stars, about 1,900 of which have already been assigned. Whenever a new star is given, the celebrity who receives it is presented with the key to Hollywood by the city's mayor. The most remarkable fact about the walk of fame, however, is that celebrities have to pay for the cost of their star! It costs almost $4,000 for each star.

The oldest museum commemorating the motion picture is on Hollywood's Sunset Boulevard. Called the Crocker Museum, it was founded by Harry Crocker in 1928. Crocker was the personal assistant to Charlie Chaplin; as a result, permanent exhibits include such priceless artifacts as Chaplin's trademark suit.

The first movie capital of America was New York. Thomas Edison founded the first movie studio there, and it was not until the early 1910s that the industry moved out to California. There are several reasons for this move. First, numerous lawsuits erupted over the patent right to the motion picture camera, so Edison needed to ship his cameras as far away from New York as possible! Second, the weather in Southern California is always beautiful, allowing for outdoor shooting year-round.

The first movie shot in Los Angeles was *The Count of Monte Christo*, directed by Francis Boggs. The first movie made in Hollywood was *In Old California*, directed by D.W. Griffith.

The first movie studio in California was the Selig Company Studios, in Edendale. The first studio in Hollywood was called the Centaur Company Studios. It was established in 1911, and it was all alone. But in 1912, over a dozen competitors moved into the area!

In terms of revenue, the biggest studio in Hollywood today is Walt Disney Studios. Disney owns Touchstone, Buena Vista, and Miramax, three smaller studios, not to mention its recent acquisition of ABC television. Disney has been responsible for creating some of the most financially successful films of the past decade, including *The Lion King* and *Pulp Fiction*. Disney also owns theme parks across the country and throughout the world!

Today, the only two studios that are still American are Warner Brothers and Disney. Universal, which was owned for many years by Japan's Matsushita Corporation, was recently sold to Canada's Seagrams. Columbia Pictures, and its sister studio TriStar, were saved from financial insolvency by Sony. Twentieth Century Fox is owned by Australia's Rupert Murdoch, a mogul much in the tradition of the earliest motion picture pioneers. Metro-Goldwyn-Mayer is owned by American businessman Kirk Kekorian, but in many ways MGM is no longer a studio. Kekorian has restructured MGM as more of an all-around entertainment company, creating resorts such as the MGM Grand in Las Vegas, rather than keeping it as a movie studio.

The first full-length feature film created in the America was *Les Miserables*, based on the French novel by Victor Hugo. The movie was only about an hour long, but this was an unprecedented amount of time to spend watching one movie in 1909. The company that produced the movie was called Vitagraph. This company has long since vanished.

Making movies, especially action movies, has always been dangerous work. Although stunt men and women are physically and mentally trained to a virtually unimaginable extent, accidents still happen. For example, both of Hollywood's productions of *Ben Hur* (a silent version was shot in 1925, and the more popular version starring Charlton Heston was shot in 1959) have resulted in numerous tragedies. During the shooting of a battle between two ships on the silent production, a fire broke out aboard one of the vessels. Several extras were killed due to smoke inhalation, and one or two drowned. During the filming of the famed chariot race in the Heston version, several camera operators fell out of a chariot and were run over by horses. Another example of a fatality resulted from shooting the aerial footage for the movie adaptation of *Catch 22*, when the assistant director's safety harness broke, and he fell out of the plane to his death.

Imagine how you would feel if you learned that each year, hundreds of the books housed in the U.S. Library of Congress were being destroyed. You would probably be outraged, as these books represent the collected knowledge of mankind. Well, rest assured that books are not being destroyed. Regrettably, however, films are. Motion picture film used to be made out of a highly volatile substance called nitrate. Nitrate is very flammable, and it literally melts if it is left in contact with air for too long. Newer types of film are made out of much more stable materials, so archives across the country are racing the clock to duplicate antique films onto the newer materials. But it is very expensive and very costly to make such duplications, so it is an uphill battle. As a result, scholars estimate that some 80% of all the black and white footage ever shot has already been lost!

We've all had the experience of going to see a movie, and being more impressed by the trailers than by the movie itself. Even the very first film makers knew the importance of trailers; they would allow audiences to view shortened versions of their movies for free in order to lure them into movie theaters. Today's Hollywood trailers cost on the order of a quarter million dollars, and every studio executive in town believes that a trailer needs to be even better than the movie it is advertising!

The average budget for a Hollywood movies these days is around $30 million. The average budget of a Hollywood movie some twenty years ago was just $5 million. So what's to blame for the rising costs? First, stars make more money now than ever before. Ten years ago, it was unheard of for any actor to make more than $5 million per film. Now, top stars like Stallone and Schwarzenegger can command $20 million. Also, the price of special effects is on the rise. New technologies, such as the computer animation used to create the mega-realistic dinosaurs in *Jurassic Park,* are extremely expensive to use. As a result, the more discriminating an audience gets, the more expensive movies become.

The average price of an adult movie ticket at a first run movie theater is $6. In large metropolitan areas, such as Los Angeles and New York, the price is $7.50. The first movie to charge an admission of $6 or more was *E.T.: The Extra-Terrestrial.* Francis Coppola once experimented with the idea of presenting newly restored classic films in huge theaters for an admission charge of $20. He hoped that by doing so, the movies would take on the artistic importance of opera or traditional theater. The experiment was a miserable failure, throwing him into heavy debt!

How do movies generate so much profit? If you ask any studio executive in Hollywood, they will all give you the same answer: merchandising. Merchandising used to be the sole domain of action movies targeted at children (i.e., the *Star Wars* line of poseable action figures). But nowadays, all movies seem to have some kind of merchandising. Take, for example, the line of "Bubba Gump" food and cookbooks that have been inspired by *Forrest Gump*. The first person to discover how much money can be made through merchandising was George Lucas, whose contracts with 20th Century Fox studios specifically indicated that he would retain the rights to all *Star Wars* merchandise. To date, that merchandise has generated over $1 billion in revenues!

The movie that has been remade the most times is *Cinderella*. Walt Disney's version of this classic tale is by far the most famous, but 93 other versions exist!

Everyone loves a good sequel—it gives you a chance to revisit some of your favorite characters, such as James Bond or Indiana Jones. The movie which has spawned the most sequels is *Dr. No*, the first Bond film. Generally, studios like to try and make sequels as quickly as possible, so that the original movie is still fresh in the audience's minds. But sometimes this is not possible. Legal disputes, for example, prevented *Return to Oz* (the sequel to *The Wizard of Oz*) from being made for approximately 40 years! *The Two Jakes*, the ill-fated sequel to the classic *Chinatown*, had to wait some twenty years before being made. In fact, a third movie in that series was planned, but it is unlikely that it will ever be produced, due to the poor box office performance of *The Two Jakes*.

The only sequel ever to win an Academy Award for Best Picture is *The Godfather, Part II*.

Everyone knows about the big bucks that today's stars can command, but the artists behind the camera can make quite a pretty penny as well. The highest paid screenwriter of all time is Joe Ezterhaus, whose screenplay for *Basic Instinct* earned him $3.6 million. James Cameron (*Terminator 2: Judgment Day, True Lies*) makes $8 to $10 million per movie. And Steven Spielberg, who takes a portion of his movies' gross profits instead of a salary, can earn up to $250 million per movie!

Some of Hollywood's best movies have been based on great books. *Gone with the Wind, Laurence of Arabia, The Graduate,* and *The Firm* are examples of novels that have successfully made the transition to the big screen. Authors like Michael Crichton and John Grisham now have multi-picture deals with studios. But, without a doubt, the author who has had the most films made based upon his work is William Shakespeare. His plays have been turned into movies over 350 times, and acclaimed Shakespearean actor/director Kenneth Branaugh is rumored to be developing a film about the playwright's life.

The first movie to show two people kissing was *The Widow Jones*, which was released in 1896. At that time, this was thought to be an extremely lude and offensive scene, and it nearly caused riots in several movie theaters. Needless to say, since then kissing has become extremely common. Who could imagine movies without romance?

We've all seen those shots in movies in which an actor seems to be standing right next to his evil twin. As most actors don't have evil twins in real life, Hollywood generally has to resort to special effects trickery in order to accomplish such shots. A piece of black card is used to cover up one half of the lens. The actor then stands in a position that can be seen through the uncovered part of the lens. The camera then rolls its film. Once this part of the shot is taken, the film is rewound to the beginning inside the camera. The piece of black card is then reversed, covering what was originally left uncovered. The actor now moves to the newly uncovered area, and the film is shot again. When it is finally projected, the actor appears to be standing next to himself.

The first Western was made in 1894 by the Thomas Edison Company. Directed by Edwin S. Porter, *The Sioux Indian Rain Dance* had a running time of approximately ten minutes. The film was shot in New Jersey! It was such a success that Porter quickly got to work making more films in a similar vain. 1895 saw the first cowboy to appear on the screen in Porter's *Bucking Broncho*.

In the early days of Hollywood, stars had contracts which allowed them to work exclusively for one studio or another. Studios frequently bartered with each other in order to get the top stars into their pictures. If, for example, Paramount wanted Shirley Temple to appear in one of their movies, they actually had to rent her services from Metro-Goldwyn-Mayer. During this period, actors had weekly salaries, rather than earning a certain sum of money per picture. A popular star from the silent era could expect to earn anywhere from $500 to $1,000 per week. The all-time champ of the silent era, however, was Mary Pickford, who earned a whopping $10,000 per week (imagine making over $500,000 a year in 1910)! Maybe Stallone isn't overpaid after all. It is rumored that the great silent comedian Harold Lloyd made $40,000 each week, but this has never been confirmed.

The highest paid actor of all time is Jack Nicholson. Learning the ropes from Lucas' success with the *Star Wars* merchandising, Nicholson opted for a cut of the revenues from *Batman*'s merchandise rather than receiving a salary. The result: a $50 million dollar payday!

Everyone knows that nepotism is a strong force in Hollywood. The Houston family, for example, has produced three generations of actors: Walter, John, and Anjelica. The Barrymores also have had a fair number grace the silver screen: Lionel, John, and even young Drew (who made her screen debut as Gertie in Steven Spielberg's *E.T.: The Extra-Terrestrial*).

It is not unusual for a big budget Hollywood feature to employ more than one camera during an action sequence. That way, many angles of the event can be achieved simultaneously, thereby making it unnecessary to restage the event. The record for the most cameras used simultaneously belongs to *Ben Hur*. During the chariot race of that film, no less than 50 cameras were hidden in the crowded audience stands!

As you may know, the first motion picture cameras did not have motors. A camera operator had to turn a crank at a steady, even pace in order to advance the film. It was not until the late 1920s that electric motors were first fitted onto cameras. They were very clunky motors, prone to breaking down at any moment, but the advent of sound necessitated them in order to avoid slight fluctuations in camera speed.

Throughout the 1930s, '40s, and '50s, the camera which dominated Hollywood was known as the Mitchell BNCR. A magnificent piece of equipment, it is still used by some cameramen today. In the 1960s, however, a new company by the name of Panavision burst onto the scene. The biggest improvement that the new company could offer over Mitchell was a reduction in the weight of the camera: Panavision's new cameras only weighed about 25 pounds, as opposed to Mitchell's 85 pounds, thereby making the hand-held shot feasible.

The fantastic point of view (POV) shot at the end of *The Exorcist*, where the priest jumps off a balcony was achieved by throwing a small camera off of the balcony!

People are rarely shown going to the bathroom in films. The first American film to feature such a scene was *Catch 22*, which was made in 1970. In other words, film had existed for nearly one hundred years before anyone had the courage to show someone going to the bathroom!

If you think Hollywood produces more movies than anywhere else in the world, then you are wrong! The cost of Hollywood movies is so high these days that it limits the number of movies that can be made there. India and Japan lead the world in terms of the number of movies produced each year, with the United States coming in third.

Studios are not the only people who finance movies these days. Individuals and companies throughout the world are lining up for their chance to participate in the Hollywood dream, financing movies with budgets reaching well over $50 million! The results of this can be disastrous. Francis Coppola at one time invested his entire net worth into the completion of *One from the Heart*. When that movie bombed at the box office, Coppola found himself $50 million in debt. On the other hand, Claude Berri made an estimated $75 million by financing *The Bear* out of his own pocket.

Test Your Movie Trivia Knowledge

1) Name all of the actors to portray James Bond in the movies.

2) Supply the last name of the following five actors: Leaf, Summer, Liberty, River, and Rainbow. (Hint: they are all related.)

3) Who was originally hired to play the role of Indiana Jones, but was unable to do so because of a contract with a weekly TV show?

4) George Lucas directed one other science fiction film before embarking on his famed *Star Wars* trilogy. What was it called?

5) Who wrote, directed, produced, and starred in the legendary movie *Citizen Kane*?

6) What two famous actors were involved in the notorious bath-house scene of *Sparatacus*, which suggested that the characters they portrayed were homosexuals? (The scene was cut from the original version of the film.)

7) Who directed the following highly controversial films: *Lolita*, *A Clockwork Orange*, and *Spartacus*?

8) What was the name of the disc jockey that Richard Dreyfuss was searching for in American Grafitti?

9) In what film does Brando utter his famous phrase: "Stella! Stella!"?

10) When did Steven Spielberg win his first Academy Award?

11) Which Hollywood studio was founded by Mary Pickford, D.W. Griffith, Charlie Chaplin, and Douglas Fairbanks, all of whom were disgruntled at their treatment by other studios?

12) What was the name of the first film to feature a dialogue soundtrack?

13) What was the name of the first feature film? (A feature film is one that runs approximately two hours or more.)

14) What is the most expensive movie ever made?

15) Who invented the movie camera?

16) Who appeared in every one of Alfred Hitchcock's films?

17) What famous Humphrey Bogart role was almost given to Ronald Reagan?

18) What two Kevin Costner films feature extensive sequences in which he speaks in a foreign language?

19) Other than Ronald Reagan, what Western movie star has made a second career out of politics?

20) Who was the only actor from the movie M*A*S*H to remain in the cast when it became a television series?

21) What was the first American movie that took over a year to make?

22) Who played the title role in *Lawrence of Arabia*?

23) What two famous stars dressed up in drag to appear in *Some Like it Hot* opposite Marilyn Monroe?

24) Who played classic rock-and-roller Jerry Lee Lewis in the movie *Great Balls of Fire*?

25) What actors portrayed escaped convicts masquerading as priests in the original and remake of *We're No Angels*?

26) Is there a movie named *Flubber*?

27) What film featured Jack Nicholson as a private investigator in pre-World War II Los Angeles?

28) What was the original name for *E.T.: The Extra-Terrestrial*?

29) In what movie did Jack Nicholson portray the Devil?

30) In what year will George Lucas release the next *Star Wars* movie?

31) *Farenheit 451*, based on the novel by Ray Bradbury, is the only English-language movie directed by what acclaimed French film maker?

32) Orson Welles' acclaimed *Citizen Kane* is based loosely on the life of what famous newspaper tycoon?

33) What role has been portrayed by both Katharine Hepburn and Winona Ryder?

34) How many women have won the Academy Award for best director?

35) What famous actress supplied the voice for E.T.?

36) What Mel Brooks' movie features Gene Wilder and Zero Mostel staging a Broadway production of a play called *Springtime for Hitler*?

37) How many roles did Peter Sellers play in *Doctor Strangelove*?

38) Who played Macauley Culkin as a baby in *Richie Rich*?

39) What was the name of James Stewart's guardian angel in *It's a Wonderful Life*?

40) What actor was "coming to dinner" in *Guess Who's Coming to Dinner*?

41) What is the name of the slapstick police department invented by silent film producer Mack Sennet?

42) What movie series featured such memorable characters as Spanky, Alfalfa, Darla, Froggy, and Buckwheat?

43) What silent film comedian is best known for performing his own daredevil stunts?

44) What Rob Reiner movie was based on the Stephen King short story *The Body*?

45) Who portrayed Frankenstein most recently on the screen?

46) How did James Dean die?

47) What star of TV's *Gilligan's Island* played Little John in *The Adventures of Robin Hood*?

48) For what organization does British secret agent James Bond work?

49) Who played Lieutenant Ripley in the terrifying science fiction movie *Alien*?

50) What is the name of the French detective played by Peter Sellars in the *Pink Panther* movies?

51) What is the Pink Panther, and where does it come from?

52) The love triangle in *The Graduate* consists of what three actors?

53) Who is Martin Sheen instructed to kill in *Apocalypse Now*?

54) *All That Jazz*, starring Roy Scheider, is loosely based on the life of what Broadway choreographer?

55) What is the highest-grossing film of all time?

56) What was the first animated movie ever to be nominated for the Best Picture Academy Award?

57) What was the first film to star both Lauren Bacall and Humphrey Bogart?

58) What actor has starred in six of the highest grossing films of all time?

59) Liza Minelli is the daughter of what famous Hollywood couple?

60) What actor turned down an Academy Award in order to protest Hollywood's negative stereotypes of Native American peoples?

61) From where did the stagecoach depart in the famous John Wayne movie *Stagecoach*?

62) What were the names of the two main characters in *The Odd Couple*, starring Walter Matthau and Jack Lemmon?

63) What controversial African-American leader did Spike Lee make a movie about?

64) Sylvester Stallone starred in what 1995 summer action movie based on a British comic strip about the lawmakers of the future?

65) What was President Kennedy's favorite movie?

66) This movie, starring Dan Aykroyd and Jane Curtin, was based on a comedy routine about aliens inhabiting the Earth first seen on television's *Saturday Night Live*.

67) This legendary producer of "B" movies gave such famous directors and actors as Francis Coppola, Martin Scorsese, and Jack Nicholson their first big breaks.

68) Johnny Depp starred in a movie biography of this man, who has been called "the worst director of all time!"

69) This Steven Spielberg movie had a scene which featured over 10,000 live snakes, some of which were poisonous.

70) This beloved Frank Capra movie starring James Stewart was originally viewed as treasonous for the disrespectful light it cast on the United States government.

71) What Walt Disney cartoon features a soundtrack made entirely of famous classical music pieces?

72) What does someone accidentally drop into a public swimming pool in the movie *Caddyshack*?

73) What star of the uproarious comedy *Animal House* went on to play the role of Mozart in *Amadeus*?

74) What is the only horror movie ever to win the Academy Award for Best Picture?

75) What movie directed by Martin Scorsese caused riots in many cities throughout the world?

76) What Woody Allen movie is based loosely on the story of *War and Peace*?

77) What "chilling" dessert is served to our heroes in *Indiana Jones and the Temple of Doom*?

78) This recent comedy was based on a *Saturday Night Live* sketch about two teenagers from Aurora, Illinois who have their own public access show on cable.

79) What was the last movie in which Natalie Wood appeared?

80) What Steve McQueen movie features a legendary car chase through the streets of San Francisco?

81) The chariot race in this epic Hollywood production was so dangerous that it caused the deaths of several stuntmen and camera operators.

82) He played Christopher Reeve's archrival, Lex Luther, in the *Superman* movies.

83) These two actors portrayed fugitives from prison in *The Defiant Ones*, a stirring film about overcoming racial tensions.

84) What is the last thing we see in the infamous shower scene of Alfred Hitchcock's *Psycho*?

85) What is the name of the motel that Janet Leigh unfortunately stumbles onto in *Psycho*?

86) In what terrifying movie does Jack Nicholson play a caretaker at a snowed-in hotel in Colorado?

87) Name the seven dwarfs.

88) What Hollywood star's real name was Archibald Alexander Leach?

89) What film features the last line: "It was beauty that killed the beast."

90) This star of such box-office hits as *Falling Down* and *Basic Instinct* produced *One Flew Over the Cuckoo's Nest*.

91) This movie documented the last album that the Beatles recorded together.

92) What child actress almost received the role of Dorothy in *The Wizard of Oz*?

93) Did Marilyn Monroe ever have plastic surgery?

94) This star of the blockbuster *Die Hard* series is married to Demi Moore, the highest paid actress of all time.

95) Did Groucho Marx ever have a real moustache during the course of his film career?

96) Name the four actors who played *The Ghostbusters*.

97) This movie about two motorcycle riders heading from Los Angeles to New Orleans has become a counter-culture classic and was one of the most successful movies of the 1960s.

98) What was the first film to employ the computer animation technique known as "morphing?"

99) What film features Mel Brooks as Moses, bringing down the Fifteen Commandments to his people (he then drops one stone tablet, resulting in only Ten Commandments remaining!)?

100) The films *Meaning of Life*, *Life of Brian*, and *The Holy Grail* were written and performed by what British comedy group?

101) What actor was originally supposed to play the tin man in *The Wizard of Oz*, but had to quit because his skin had an allergic reaction to all of the makeup?

102) What is Rick's (Humphrey Bogart's) last name in *Casablanca*?

103) What 1946 movie was remade as the musical *The King and I* in 1956?

104) What do the movies *Freakie Friday*, *Vice Versa*, and *Like Father, Like Son* have in common?

105) What Tom Wolfe book was bought by a Hollywood producer to make into a movie for the unheard of sum of $5 million (the movie was a disastrous flop)?

106) What was the name of the Motown remake of *The Wizard of Oz*?

107) On what book was D.W. Griffith's epic *The Birth of a Nation* based?

108) What actor were all five of the following women married to at one point: Dyan Cannon, Virginia Cherrill, Betsy Drake, Barbara Harris, and Barbara Hutton?

109) What silver screen comedian was married to Gilda Radner?

110) Who garnered lots of bad publicity throughout the 1980s by colorizing some of Hollywood's black and white classics?

111) Who helped write the screenplay for *Citizen Kane*, but did not receive credit as a screenwriter (hint: he starred in the TV series *The Paper Chase*)?

112) What famous baseball player starred in the little-seen 1938 movie called *Rawhide*?

113) What two characters did Charlton Heston play in *The Ten Commandments*?

114) Name all of the brides and all of the brothers in *Seven Brides for Seven Brothers*.

115) Who coined the term "MacGuffin," which means a plot device that propels the story forward? In *Citizen Kane*, for example, the MacGuffin would be Rosebud.

116) What are the names of the two sleds in *Citizen Kane*?

117) What was Cinerama?

118) In what film did Robert Redford play a star hitter for the New York Knights?

119) What movie was originally called *The Three Thousand Dollar a Week Date*?

120) What movie is about the trials and tribulations of the crew of the U.S.S. Reluctant?

121) What movie role has been played by both Bill Murray and Jack Nicholson?

122) What Charlton Heston film required almost one-third of its entire budget to be devoted to makeup?

123) How many times did Rocky Balboa fight against Apollo Creed in the *Rocky* films?

124) In what Biblical epic did John Wayne appear?

125) How much money does Robert Redford offer Woody Harrelson for one night with his wife (Demi Moore) in *Indecent Proposal*?

126) What famous movie monster was designed by special effects artist Eiji Tsubuyara?

127) Who was originally cast in the lead role of *The Jazz Singer*?

128) Who played the lead in the late-1970s remake of *The Jazz Singer*?

129) Name all of Martin Scorsese's films that have starred Robert De Niro.

130) What famous American playwright has gone on to direct such films as *House of Games* and *Homicide*.

131) What Vietnam war movie was based loosely on Joseph Conrad's *Heart of Darkness*, about 19th century slave traders in the African Congo?

132) During the late-1960s and early-1970s, many Westerns were made in Italy. What are these Westerns commonly called?

133) *The Magnificent Seven*, a Western starring Steve McQueen and Yul Brynner, is based on what Akira Kurosawa movie?

134) Who played the voice of John Smith in Disney's latest animated blockbuster, *Pocahontas*?

135) What actor from TV's *In Living Cover* found astronomical fame and fortune after appearing in *The Mask*?

136) What star of *Easy Rider* also appeared in the Keanu Reeves action thriller *Speed*?

137) What movie did acclaimed actor Warren Beatty direct and star in that was based on an old comic book character?

138) What movie featured Dudley Moore as a rich, alcoholic race car driver?

139) *Blade Runner*, starring Harrison Ford as a cop in a futuristic society threatened by robots, was based on what classic science fiction novel?

140) Philip K. Dick's famous novella *We Can Remember it for You Wholesale* was turned into what science fiction movie starring Arnold Schwarzenegger?

141) What is the only movie in which Henry Fonda starred as the bad guy?

142) What movie by John Boorman is based on the Arthurian legend of Great Britain?

143) For what film did Dustin Hoffman have to take stand-up comedy lessons in order to play the lead role?

144) What are the three fabled religious artifacts that Indiana Jones has sought out in his silver screen exploits?

145) How are John Houston and Faye Dunaway supposed to be related in the movie *Chinatown*? How does this cause a great deal of tension?

146) What hit movie starring Donald Sutherland and Elliot Gould spawned the most successful TV comedy series of all time?

147) What three letters constitute the recall code prefix for planes armed with nuclear warheads in *Dr. Strangelove*, and what do these letters stand for?

148) What are the names of the two most prominent motion-picture camera companies in the world today?

149) What does Charlton Heston discover at the end of *The Planet of the Apes*, indicating that he is still on Earth?

150) Where do Sylvester Stallone and Armand Assante have their final showdown in *Judge Dredd*, a futuristic action thriller based on a British comic book?

151) What film features Robin Williams as a jazz-loving Russian saxophonist who defects to America?

152) How many times does Dustin Hoffman cry out "Elaine!" at the end of *The Graduate*?

153) What Italian carmaker renamed its most popular model after *The Graduate*, as this car figured prominently in the action of that movie?

154) The Ruby Slippers in *The Wizard of Oz* were originally what color (they were changed because red looked much better in the new creation of color film)?

155) What is the name of the rarely-seen sequel to *The Wizard of Oz*?

156) What Roman Polanski thriller features Harrison Ford as an American tourist in France whose wife is mistaken for a spy and kidnapped?

157) What Alfred Hitchcock movie was originally going to be called *The Man on Lincoln's Nose*.

158) Name all four of Vito Corleone's sons in *The Godfather*.

159) What special occasion is the backdrop for the opening scenes of *The Godfather*?

160) Name all four actors who have played the Godfather in *The Godfather* movies.

161) What movie directed by David Lynch is based on the classic science fiction novel by Frank Herbert?

162) How many times do we see Darth Vader strangle someone in the *Star Wars* movies?

163) Name the debut movie directed by ex-video store clerk Quentin Tarantino.

164) Robert Rodriguez caused a sensation in Hollywood in 1993 when he made what feature-length movie for just $7,000?

165) What well-known master of "B" movies wrote an autobiography entitled *How I Made A Hundred Movies in Hollywood Without Losing a Dime*?

166) In what movie did Gregory Peck star as a lawyer in the deep South defending

a wrongly accused African American man against the charge of rape?

167) In what movie does Harrison Ford play Dr. Richard Kimble, a man wrongly accused of murdering his wife? (Hint: this movie is based on a popular 1960s TV show.)

168) What is the nickname of the man who actually killed Dr. Kimble's wife in the movie referred to in Question #167?

169) What fabled place are Kevin Costner and his water-logged companions searching for in *Waterworld*?

170) What movie features Dustin Hoffman fighting against an experimental bacterial weapon that is accidentally released into a small town in Northern California?

171) What is "the stuff that dreams are made of"?

172) What was the name of Humphrey Bogart's boat in *The African Queen*?

173) Which Frank Capra movie featured James Stewart as all-American hero Jefferson Smith?

174) Name the Kurt Russell movie in which all of Manhattan Island is turned into a maximum security prison in the near future.

175) In the John Carpenter thriller *The Thing*, the thing is an alien that can disguise itself as any type of life form. Name the animal that we first see it disguised as.

176) What kind of snakes guarded the Ark of the Covenant in *Raiders of the Lost Ark*?

177) In *Indiana Jones and the Last Crusade*, we discover that Indiana is only a nickname. What is Indiana's real name?

178) In *The Miracle of Morgan's Creek*, what is the miracle?

179) What Arnold Schwarzenegger action

picture focused on a group of U.S. Commandos being hunted by an invisible alien in the South American rain forests?

180) He went from being a teen idol on TV's *21 Jump Street* to being a respected film actor in such hits as *Benny and Joon* and *What's Eating Gilbert Grape*.

181) On what island do we first discover King Kong?

182) Were all of the dinosaurs on Jurassic Park supposed to be male or female?

183) In *Close Encounters of the Third Kind*, what famous luxury liner mysteriously turns up in the middle of the Gobi Desert?

184) What famous comedy duo brought their "Who's on First" routine to the silver screen?

185) Why do both Allied and Axis supporters visit Casablanca in the film of the same name?

186) What is the first type of dinosaur to kill someone in *Jurassic Park*?

187) What was E.T.'s occupation?

188) This biography of Charles Lindbergh, starring James Stewart, draws its title from the name of the plane in which the famous aviator first crossed the Atlantic Ocean.

189) Name the trilogy of Spaghetti Westerns starring Clint Eastwood as a gunfighter with no name.

190) The crew of the space shuttle presented an honorary Academy Award to this popular science fiction film maker.

191) What Tom Hanks' film chronicled an actual disaster that occurred during one of America's moon missions?

192) Kurt Russell and William Baldwin starred in this Ron Howard thriller about Chicago firefighters battling against a mysterious arsonist.

193) Who committed the *Murder on the Orient Express*?

194) This psychological thriller about two murderous homosexual playwrights starred Michael Caine and Christopher Reeve.

195) David Lynch revealed the events leading up to the murder of Laura Palmer in this movie, which took place before the TV show of the same name.

196) What comedy-thriller followed one day in the life of hit men John Travolta and Samuel L. Jackson?

197) Bruce Willis' first foray onto the silver screen was in this uproarious comedy directed by Blake Edwards, co-starring Kim Bassinger and John Larroquette.

198) To whom is the movie *The Great Escape* dedicated?

199) Which James Bond film takes place predominately in Japan?

200) Which James Bond Film features a sports car that turns into a submarine?

201) What is the name of the newsreel that opens *Citizen Kane*?

202) What movie stars Jon Voight and Dustin Hoffman as small-time hustlers in New York City?

203) What movie starring Darryl Hannah and Tom Hanks centered on a love story between a man and a mermaid?

204) Eric Bogosian starred in this Oliver Stone film about a Howard Stern-like radio show host who is murdered because of his radical views.

205) What silent epic by D.W. Griffith discussed racism as it occurred throughout many different eras in the history of human civilization?

206) This comedy starred Charles Chaplin as a Hitler-like leader.

207) This African American actor, best known for his performance as Lando Calrissian in the *Star Wars* movies, starred in *Lady Sings the Blues* opposite Diana Ross.

208) What popular singer of the 1980s starred opposite Mel Gibson in *Mad Max: Beyond Thunderdome*?

209) The classic action films *The Guns of Navarone* and *Ice Station Zebra* are based on the novels by what famous British author?

210) This famous Scottish actor portrayed Captain Marco Ramius, the Russian submarine commander, in *The Hunt for Red October*.

211) Who played the title role in David Lynch's *The Elephant Man*?

212) This young actor, who starred in such hits as *The Breakfast Club* and *Young Guns*, is Martin Sheen's son and Charlie Sheen's brother.

213) These two actors, who were once married to each other, starred as lovers in *The Fly*, a movie about a scientific experiment that goes awry.

214) What actress starred opposite Richard Gere in *Pretty Woman*, catapulting her into the status of superstar?

215) Name the three movies that James Dean completed before his untimely death.

216) Name the movie in which Bob Hoskins stars as a private detective trying to solve the murder of a cartoon character.

217) Who is the only patient to escape from the mental ward at the end of *One Flew Over the Cuckoo's Nest*?

218) Who has been nominated for the most Academy Awards?

219) Who has won the most Academy Awards?

220) When were the first Academy Awards held?

221) She won an Academy Award for her performance in *The Diary of Anne Frank*.

222) Who is the youngest actress ever to win the Academy Award?

223) Henry Fonda starred as Tom Joad in this John Huston adaptation of the classic by John Steinbeck.

224) In what country are Sylvester Stallone and Jerry Lewis considered national heroes for their contributions to the art of film?

225) Name the movie in which Tony Curtis starred as the greatest magician of all time.

Trivia Answers

1) Sean Connery, George Lazenby, Roger Moore, Timothy Dalton, Pierce Brosnan, and David Niven. Peter Sellers played a man masquerading as James Bond, and Woody Allen once played his insane nephew, Jimmy Bond.

2) Phoenix.

3) Tom Selleck. He had to turn the role down because producers would not let him out of his *Magnum, P.I.* contract.

4) *THX 1138*.

5) Orson Welles.

6) Sir Laurence Olivier and Tony Curtis.

7) Stanley Kubrick.

8) Wolfman Jack. He was played by Wolfman Jack.

9) *A Streetcar Named Desire*.

10) 1993.

11) United Artists.

12) *The Jazz Singer*.

13) *The Birth of a Nation*.

14) *Waterworld*. (The price tag for making this Kevin Costner action film is somewhere between $175 and $220 million!)

15) There are many conflicting reports on who actually invented the device, but Thomas Edison held the first patent for a movie camera in the United States.

16) Alfred Hitchcock.

17) Rick Blaine from *Casablanca*.

18) *Dances with Wolves* (he speaks Sioux Lacota); *Waterworld* (he speaks an imaginary future language).

19) Clint Eastwood.

20) Gary Burghoff, who played Corporal Radar O'Reilly.

21) Charlie Chaplin's *The Kid*.

22) Peter O'Toole.

23) Tony Curtis and Jack Lemmon.

24) Dennis Quaid.

25) Humphrey Bogart, Peter Ustinov, and Aldo Ray starred in the original. Sean Penn and Robert De Niro starred in the remake.

26) No. The movie that most people mistakenly call *Flubber* is *The Absent-Minded Professor*, starring Fred MacMurray.

27) *Chinatown*.

28) *A Boy's Life*.

29) *The Witches of Eastwick*.

30) 1998.

31) Francois Truffaut.

32) William Randolph Hearst.

33) Jo March in *Little Women*.

34) Zero.

35) Debra Winger.

36) *The Producers*.

37) Three: President Merkin Muffley, Group-Captain Lionel Mandrake, and the infamous Dr. Strangelove himself.

38) Kierin Culkin, Macauley's little brother.

39) Clarence.

40) Sidney Poitier.

41) The Keystone Kops.

42) The *Our Gang* movies. The series was renamed *The Little Rascals* when it was shown on television.

43) Harold Lloyd.

44) *Stand By Me*.

45) Kenneth Branaugh played Baron Victor Frankenstein. Robert De Niro played Frankenstein's monster.

46) In a car crash.

47) Alan Hale ("Skipper").

48) MI6.

49) Sigourney Weaver.

50) Inspector Clouseau.

51) A priceless jewel. It is the national treasure of the fictitious country of Lugache.

52) Dustin Hoffman, Anne Bancroft, and Katharine Ross.

53) Kurtz, played by Marlon Brando.

54) Bob Fosse.

55) Steven Spielberg's *Jurassic Park*.

56) Walt Disney's *Beauty and the Beast*.

57) *To Have and Have Not*.

58) Harrison Ford, who has appeared in all three *Star Wars* and all three *Indiana Jones* movies. He also had a small role in *E.T.: The Extre-Terrestrial*, but it was cut out before the movie was released.

59) Vincente Minneli and Judy Garland.

60) Marlon Brando.

61) Tonto, New Mexico.

62) Oscar Madison and Felix Ungar.

63) Malcolm X.

64) *Judge Dredd*.

65) *The Manchurian Candidate*.

66) *The Coneheads*.

67) Roger Corman.

68) Ed Wood.

69) *Raiders of the Lost Ark*.

70) *Mr. Smith Goes to Washington*.

71) *Fantasia*.

72) A candy bar.

73) Tom Hulce.

74) *The Silence of the Lambs*.

75) *The Last Temptation of Christ*

76) *Love and Death*.

77) Chilled monkey brains.

78) *Wayne's World*.

79) *Brainstorm*.

80) *Bullitt.*

81) *Ben-Hur.*

82) Gene Hackman.

83) Tony Curtis and Sidney Poitier.

84) Blood running down the drain.

85) The Bates Motel.

86) *The Shining.*

87) Sleepy, Dopey, Happy, Bashful, Grumpy, Sneezy, and Doc.

88) Cary Grant.

89) *King Kong.*

90) Michael Douglas.

91) *Let it Be.*

92) Shirley Temple.

93) Yes, when she was 23 years old.

94) Bruce Willis.

95) No.

96) Bill Murray, Dan Aykroyd, Harold Ramis, and Ernie Hudson.

97) *Easy Rider*.

98) *Willow*.

99) *History of the World, Part I*

100) Monty Python.

101) Buddy Epson.

102) Blaine.

103) *Anna and the King of Siam*.

104) All are about a parent trading bodies with a child.

105) *Bonfire of the Vanities*.

106) *The Wiz.*

107) *The Klansmen*, by Thomas Dixon, Jr.

108) Cary Grant.

109) Gene Wilder.

110) Ted Turner.

111) John Houseman.

112) Lou Gehrig.

113) Moses and the voice of God.

114) Alice, Dorcas, Liza, Martha, Milly, Ruth, Sarah, Adam, Benjamin, Caleb, Daniel, Ephraim, Frank, and Gideon.

115) Alfred Hitchcock.

116) Rosebud and Avenger.

117) An old-fashioned widescreen process that required three-movie cameras to be run simultaneously.

118) *The Natural*.

119) *Pretty Woman*. The producers felt this was a catchier title, but they retained the storyline of Richard Gere hiring Julia Roberts to be his week-long date for $3,000.

120) *Mister Roberts*.

121) Both actors played a massochistic dental patient in different versions of *The Little Shop of Horrors*. The patient did not have a name in either production.

122) *The Planet of the Apes*.

123) Three. In *Rocky I* and *Rocky II*, their fight comprised the climax of the movie. In *Rocky III*, the two characters had a secret rematch at the end of the movie after Rocky had defeated Clubber Lang.

124) *The Greatest Story Ever Told*. He played a Roman Centurion.

125) $1 million.

126) Godzilla.

127) George Jessell.

128) Neil Diamond.

129) *Mean Streets, Taxi Driver, New York, New York, Raging Bull, The King of Comedy, Goodfellas*, and *Cape Fear*.

130) David Mamet.

131) *Apocalypse Now*.

132) Spaghetti Westerns.

133) *The Seven Samurai*.

134) Mel Gibson.

135) Jim Carrey.

136) Dennis Hopper.

137) *Dick Tracy*.

138) *Arthur*.

139) *Do Androids Dream of Electric Sheep*, by Philip K. Dick.

140) *Total Recall*.

141) *Once Upon a Time in the West*. He plays Frank, a character so evil that he actually shoots an unarmed child for no reason whatsoever!

142) *Excalibur*.

143) *Lenny*. Hoffman played controversial stand-up comedian Lenny Bruce in this tragic biography directed by Bob Fosse.

144) The Ark of the Covenant (in *Raiders of the Lost Ark*), the Sankara Stones (in *Indiana Jones and the Temple of Doom*), and the Holy Grail (in *Indiana Jones and the Last Crusade*).

145) Dunaway was Houston's daughter and his unwilling lover. Houston's character, Mulwray, was supposed to have raped Dunaway while she was still in her teens.

146) *M*A*S*H*.

147) P.O.E. The letters stand either for "Peace On Earth" or "Purity of Essence," two favorite sayings of the insane General Jack D. Ripper.

148) Panavision, an American company, and Arriflex, a German company.

149) The remnants of the Statue of Liberty.

150) Inside the Statue of Liberty.

151) *Moscow on the Hudson.*

152) Twenty-seven.

153) Alfa Romeo.

154) Silver.

155) *Return to Oz.*

156) *Frantic.*

157) *North by Northwest.*

158) Sonny, Fredo, Michael, and Tom Hagen, his adopted son.

159) The wedding of Vito Corleone's daughter.

160) Robert De Niro, Marlon Brando, Al Pacino, and Andy Garcia.

161) *Dune.*

162) Three.

163) *Reservoir Dogs.*

164) *El Mariachi.*

165) Roger Corman.

166) *To Kill a Mockingbird.*

167) *The Fugitive.*

168) "The One-Armed Man."

169) Dry Land.

170) *Outbreak*.

171) The Maltese Falcon.

172) The African Queen.

173) *Mr. Smith Goes to Washington*.

174) *Escape from New York*.

175) A husky.

176) Asps.

177) Henry Jones, Jr.

178) The birth of sextuplets.

179) *Predator*.

180) Johnny Depp.

181) Skull Island.

182) Female.

183) The Titanic.

184) Abbott and Costello.

185) Because it is neutral territory.

186) Velociraptor.

187) Botanist.

188) *The Spirit of St. Louis*.

189) *A Fistful of Dollars, For a Few Dollars More*, and *The Good, the Bad, and the Ugly*.

190) George Lucas.

191) *Apollo 13*.

192) *Backdraft*.

193) All of the passengers conspired together to commit the murder.

194) *Deathtrap*.

195) *Twin Peaks: Fire Walk With Me*.

196) *Pulp Fiction*.

197) *Blind Date*.

198) "The fifty." *The Great Escape* is based on an actual prisoner of war escape that took place during World War II. The Nazis managed to recapture most of the escapees, fifty of whom they executed as examples.

199) *You Only Live Twice*.

200) *The Spy Who Loved Me*.

201) "News on the March."

202) *Midnight Cowboy*.

203) *Splash*.

204) *Talk Radio*.

205) *Intolerance*.

206) *The Great Dictator*.

207) Billy Dee Williams.

208) Tina Turner.

209) Alistair Maclean.

210) Sean Connery.

211) John Hurt.

212) Emilio Estevez.

213) Jeff Goldblum and Geena Davis.

214) Julia Roberts.

215) *Rebel Without a Cause, Giant,* and *East of Eden*.

216) *Who Framed Roger Rabbit?*

217) The Chief.

218) Edith Head, a costume designer.

219) Edith Head.

220) 1929.

221) Shelley Winters.

222) Tatum O'Neil.

223) *The Grapes of Wrath.*

224) France.

225) *Houdini.*